THE HALLOWEEN BOOK

ANNALEES LIM

FRANKLIN WATTS
LONDON·SYDNEY

FRANKLIN WATTS
First published in Great Britain in 2017 by The Watts Publishing Group
Copyright © The Watts Publishing Group, 2017
All rights reserved.

Editor: Sarah Silver
Design: Square and Circus
Illustrations: Supriya Sahai

HB ISBN 978 1 4451 5241 7
PB ISBN 978 1 4451 5242 4

Picture credits: Benophotography/Shutterstock: 5c. Linda Bucklin/
Dreamstime: 4-5 bg. Daniel Dempster/Alamy: 4b. Kudryashka/
Shutterstock: 15b. Au Ho Leung/Dreamstime: 21lb. Shutterstock: 22-23,
24-25. Solstock/istockphoto: 8b. Natalie Speers Uerfmann/Shutterstock:
11b. vladgphoto/Shutterstock: 5b. yWww78/CC Wikimedia Commons.
National Register of Historic Places in Robertson County, Tennessee: 7b.
Additional illustrations: Freepik

Every attempt has been made to clear copyright. Should there be any
inadvertent omission please apply to the publisher for rectification.

MIX
Paper from
responsible sources
FSC
www.fsc.org   FSC® C104740

Printed in China

Franklin Watts
An imprint of
Hachette Children's Group
Part of The Watts Publishing Group
Carmelite House
50 Victoria Embankment
London EC4Y 0DZ

An Hachette UK Company
www.hachette.co.uk

www.franklinwatts.co.uk

SPIDER HUNT

Can you spot the ten spiders
that are hidden in the
pages of this book.
HINT: they all look
like this one, so
keep your eyes peeled
for these eight-legged
creatures.

CONTENTS

WHAT IS HALLOWEEN?

Every year on 31 October, we celebrate the spooky festival of Halloween. We dress up, go trick-or-treating and play special games. But what is Halloween and why do we celebrate it?

Samhain

Halloween is thought to come from the old Celtic (Scottish and Irish) festival of Samhain, which celebrated the end of summer and the beginning of winter. People believed that at this time of year, the worlds of the living and the dead came closest together. Ghosts and creatures with magical powers, such as witches, came to life. To drive them away, people held parties where they lit huge bonfires. They also dressed in scary animal costumes!

Why is it called Halloween?

Since the 9th century CE, 1 November has been known as All Saints' or All Hallows' Day. This is a day when Christians remember dead people who did good things during their lifetime (saints). The night before All Hallows' Day was known as All Hallows' Eve, which was shortened to Hallowe'en, now spelt Halloween.

Halloween traditions

During the 19th century, Scottish and Irish immigrants to the USA introduced the festival to their new home. Today, Halloween is celebrated all around the world. Lots of Halloween traditions, such as dressing up, trick-or-treating and even carving pumpkins, have been passed down to us over hundreds of years.

THE LEGEND OF JACK-O'-LANTERN

According to Irish legend, Jack was a mean old man who loved playing tricks on people. One day, he even tricked the devil into climbing an apple tree. Jack hurriedly placed crosses around the trunk of the tree. Unable to touch a cross, the devil was stuck in the tree. Before removing the crosses, Jack made the devil promise him not to take Jack's soul when he died.

Many years later, when Jack finally died, he was not allowed to enter heaven as he had led such a wicked life. So Jack went down to hell and the devil. But the devil kept his promise and would not allow him to enter hell. Now Jack could do nothing but wander forever between heaven and hell. He asked the devil how he could leave, as there was no light. The devil tossed him an ember to help Jack light his way. Jack had a turnip with him. He hollowed it out and placed the ember inside. From that day Jack roamed the earth without a resting place, lighting his way as he went with his turnip 'jack-o'-lantern'.

At Halloween, Irish people hollowed out turnips, potatoes and sugarbeets. They placed a light in them to ward off evil spirits and keep Jack away. In the 19th century, Irish immigrants to the USA discovered that pumpkins were bigger and easier to carve out, so they used them instead.

A HALLOWEEN GHOST STORY

The Bell Witch Cave, USA

"Welcome to the Bell Witch Cave!" announced our guide. "Strange things have been happening here in Adams, Tennessee since 1817. This is the mouth of the cave where the ghost of Kate is said to enter and depart this world."

My parents and I walked down a long winding tunnel that got narrower the further we went. Reaching an opening, the faint yellow glow of the lightbulbs lit up the limestone walls of the cave. I looked back into the darkness of the tunnel behind me and shivered. Shadows of the stalactites closed in on me from above, making me duck as I walked towards the group.

Excited whispers of people awaiting more tales of Kate filled the cave ... but one whisper stood out.

The eerie voice was getting louder, drawing me in towards it until I was far from everyone. Soon it was so loud I had to cover my ears. How could no one else hear it?

Suddenly the face of an old woman appeared on the cave wall in front of me. I stepped backwards with fear but billows of black fog emerged, forcing me forwards into the wall. Fog circled around me so close that my chest tightened. I couldn't breathe. I couldn't even scream.

I closed my eyes as tight as I could, wishing it all would stop.

Something grasped my shoulders. I started to shake, unsure if it was from fear or the Bell Witch herself. Then there was silence.

I felt like I was woken up from a deep sleep. Opening my eyes I saw my parents standing over me; it was my father who was shaking me awake. But something suddenly caught my eye. I looked over my dad's shoulder just in time to see the last few wisps of black fog disappear into the black of the tunnel.

NOT JUST A STORY

The Bell Witch Cave is in Tennessee, USA. The Bell family were tormented by ghosts from 1817 until 1821, and many believe Kate still haunts the place today.

TRICK-OR-TREATING

Why do we go trick-or-treating?

Trick-or-treating is a fun Halloween activity. Children dress up and knock on people's doors and say 'trick or treat' to receive sweets and chocolates. People have been doing similar things since long before Halloween existed. Guising was first recorded at Halloween in Scotland in 1895. Children dressed up in disguises and visited people's homes to collect food or money.

Get ready!

You can have so much fun trick-or-treating with your friends and family. Have a look at this tick list to make sure you have everything planned before your big adventure out!

1. **Stay safe** Make sure you bring an adult with you. They will make sure you don't get lost and can help carry all the treats you have collected.

2. **Knock knock!** Not everyone celebrates Halloween so only visit the houses of people that you know.

3. **Bright idea** If it is dark when you start trick-or-treating, take a lantern (see the craft idea opposite) or bring a torch.

4. **Take care** Don't stand too close to pumpkins and candles or your costume might catch fire.

MONSTER BAG

Keep all your sweets safe with this mighty monster bag, complete with sharp teeth to stop prying hands from taking your treats!

YOU WILL NEED:
- brown paper bag
- black marker pen
- scissors
- white and coloured card
- glue stick

STEP 1
Fold over the top quarter of the paper bag and use the black marker pen to colour in a black 'D' shape on its side for the mouth, just under the fold.

STEP 2
Cut out some white triangles, two horns and two circles, drawing some black dots on the circles to make the eyes. Glue the triangles onto the mouth shape to make rows of teeth.

STEP 3
Cut out some arms using the coloured card. Stick the arms and the horns onto each side of the bag.

LED LANTERN

Light you way in the dark with this illuminated ghoul lantern made from recycled yoghurt pots.

YOU WILL NEED:
- 2 yoghurt pots (clear semi-translucent)
- permanent black marker pen
- scissors
- sticky tape
- ribbon or string
- LED candle

STEP 1
Draw a ghostly face onto one of the yoghurt pots using the permanent black marker pen.

STEP 2
Cut out two fin shapes and a tail from the other yoghurt pot. Stick these onto the first pot using sticky tape.

STEP 3
Make two small holes on each side of the top of the pot. Tie some ribbon or string around the top to make a handle.

CLEVER COSTUMES

During Samhain (see page 4) people dressed up as ghouls in order to trick the spirits so they would not get haunted by them. Try dressing up as these spooky characters to trick the spirits at Halloween.

YOU WILL NEED:
- black t-shirt
- newspaper
- black gloves
- white chalk
- white acrylic paint
- paint brush

Skeleton costume

STEP 1
Put some newspaper inside the gloves and t-shirt so that the paint doesn't go through the fabric.

STEP 2
Use the white chalk to draw bone shapes onto the gloves and t-shirt.

STEP 3
Colour in the chalk shapes with one thin layer of paint. Leave to dry in a warm place before you remove the newspaper.

Day of the Dead mask

YOU WILL NEED:

- a cereal box
- scissors
- white paint
- paint brush
- pencil
- felt-tip pens
- hole punch
- ribbon

STEP 1

Cut out the front of the cereal box so you have a flat piece of card and paint it white.

STEP 2

When the paint is dry, draw a skull shape with eye holes and cut it out.

STEP 3

Draw on fancy patterns using the felt-tip pens.

STEP 4

Punch a hole on each side and attach the ribbon so you can wear the mask.

Did you KNOW?

Mexico celebrates a similar holiday to Halloween called the Day of the Dead. They honour the dead by creating altars that are stacked with gifts like food, flowers and highly decorated sugar skulls.

FRIGHTENING FANCY DRESS

Disguise your head and transform yourself into a scary creature with these fancy dress costumes.

Frankenstein's monster

STEP 1
Cut the top and bottom off the cereal box.

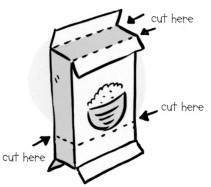

cut here

cut here

cut here

STEP 2
Bend the card into a tube and make sure it fits your head. Make it smaller if necessary by cutting one side and re-joining with sticky tape.

YOU WILL NEED:
- a cereal box
- sticky tape
- scissors
- green and black paint
- paint brushes
- aluminium foil

STEP 3
Cut triangle shapes along the top of the box to make the hair. Paint this black and the rest green.

STEP 4
Shape some aluminium foil into bolts and tape them to each side.

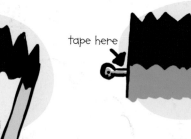

tape here

tape here

👉 **TOP TIP!**

To complete your costume, put on green face paint and cut jagged edges into an old, dark-coloured t-shirt.

Werewolf

YOU WILL NEED:
- grey fake fur fabric
- scissors
- fabric glue
- black felt
- headband

STEP 1
Cut out four triangles and a long nose from grey fake fur fabric.

STEP 2
Glue two triangles of fabric together to make an ear. Repeat to make two ears.

glue here   glue here

STEP 3
Cut out a triangle from the black felt and glue it to the fur nose shape.

STEP 4
Stick all the pieces onto the headband.

☞ TOP TIP!
Cover a pair of old gloves with some leftover fur! Make sharp claws by sticking on triangle-shaped nails from yellow felt.

How do monsters tell their future?
They read their horrorscope!

Did you KNOW?
Mumming was a medieval custom from Europe to celebrate feast days in the Christian calendar. People dressed up as different characters and performed dances and plays, going from house to house for each performance.

THROW A GREAT HALLOWEEN PARTY

There's no better way to celebrate this haunted holiday season than with a party for all your friends and family. There can be lots of things to plan so follow this perfect party tick list to impress your ghoulish guests!

2.
DECIDE ON A THEME

Picking a theme for your party can help make choosing decorations, food and costumes a bit easier! If you are stuck for ideas, try using our decoration ideas on pages 20-27 to create a Haunted House, Zombie Graveyard, Dracula's Castle or Monster Mash Ball!

1.
INVITATIONS

People will need to know all about your party so that they turn up at the right time and the right place. Use this example to help you remember all the important details to tell people!

You are invited to my
SPOOKTACULAR
HALLOWEEN
PARTY!

Time | Date | Address | Dress code | RSVP

3.
DECORATIONS

Making all your decorations by hand is a cheap and easy way to transform your house, inside and out. Invite some friends around before the big day to help create lots of terrifying things for you to use.

4.
FIENDISH FOOD

Your party guests will be peckish so take some time to cook up a storm using the recipes on page 16.

5.
PACK A PUNCH

Devilish drinks will help make your party complete. Create fruit punches with green or purple juices and add peeled grapes to look like eyeballs. Serve in a large pot to look like you have brewed your punch in a witch's cauldron.

6.
GAMES

Plan some fun activities for your guests to join in with when they arrive. There are lots of ideas on page 18. Make your party even scarier by playing games in dimmed light or with torches. You could even choose to make lots of LED lanterns like the ones on page 9.

Did you KNOW?

Black and orange are the colours that are most associated with Halloween! This tradition dates back to pagan times. Orange represents autmn leaves and the harvest. Black symbolises the death of the summer.

FIENDISH FOOD

Use these easy-to-follow recipes to create impressive bakes for your party guests! These also make perfect ghoulish goodies to give out to any trick-or-treaters that come knocking.

Gingerbread zombies

YOU WILL NEED:
- gingerbread men
- grey icing
- spoon
- raisins
- icing pens

STEP 1
Buy or make some gingerbread men. Spoon on some grey icing to cover the surface.

STEP 2
Press some raisins into the icing to make eyes.

Did you KNOW?

The Christian practice of souling dates back to the medieval times in England. A small round cake, called a soul cake, was served during All Hallows' Eve, All Saints' Day and All Souls' Day. It would be given out to the 'soulers' who went from house to house to sing to commemorate the dead.

STEP 3
Once the icing has set, use icing pens to decorate the body. Use black to give some of them a grimacing mouth. The clothes will need to be tattered looking so use lots of jagged edges, and remember to use red icing for blood!

Cupcake decorating

STEP 1
Use some jam as glue, and stick a marshmallow onto the top of the cupcake.

STEP 2
Roll out some white fondant icing and use a cookie cutter to cut out a circle.

STEP 3
Cover the marshmallow in jam and stick the fondant circle on top.

STEP 4
Draw in a ghost face with an icing pen.

FOR THE GHOST YOU WILL NEED:
- plain cupcakes
- jam
- a marshmallow
- fondant icing
- rolling pin
- cookie cutter
- black icing pen

STEP 1
Pipe a mound of green icing onto the top of the cupcake. Place a biscuit onto the top of the icing to make the head and draw on eyes with an icing pen.

STEP 2
Break one biscuit in half for the wings, and one into quarters for the ears. Draw on wing and ear details with an icing pen.

STEP 3
Place one wing on either side of the head and stick the ears into the icing behind the head.

FOR THE BAT YOU WILL NEED:
- plain cupcakes
- green butter icing
- piping bag
- chocolate biscuits
- white icing pen

PARTY GAMES

You don't have to throw a party to enjoy playing these fun-to-make Halloween games. You can play on your own or challenge your friends and family — remember to keep score!

Pin the hat onto the witch

YOU WILL NEED:
- a large piece of card
- felt-tip pens
- black card
- scissors
- stickers
- Blu-tack
- long scarf

STEP 1
Draw a witch's head in the centre of a piece of card.

STEP 2
Cut out a hat shape from the black card and decorate with stickers. Each player in the game can make and decorate their own.

STEP 3
Put some Blu-tack behind each hat you have made.

STEP 4
Use a scarf as a blindfold and spin the first player around. Guide them towards the witch drawing that is stuck on a wall.

Get them to stick their hat on the wall. The winner is the player who gets their hat the closest to the top of the witch's head!

Black cat bowling

YOU WILL NEED:
- five cardboard tubes (from kitchen roll)
- scissors
- black paint
- paint brush
- coloured card
- felt tip pens
- glue stick
- a soft ball

STEP 1
Cut each tube in half so you have ten tubes. Press in the tops of the tubes to make the cats' ears.

press down here

STEP 2
Paint them black and leave to dry.

STEP 3
Cut eyes, nose and whiskers from the coloured card and decorate with felt-tip pens. Glue onto the painted tubes to give each cat a face.

STEP 4
Line the cats up in a bowling pin formation. Take turns to try and knock them down with a soft ball.

What do you call a witch's garage?
A broom closet.

Did you KNOW?
People who celebrated Samhain honoured a pagan goddess called the Crone, which means the old one or earth mother, who collected souls in a giant pot. Over the years this image has been transformed into the witch we see today.

HAUNTED HOUSE

These two crafts will get you started to help transform any room of your house into a haunted hotspot for ghosts and ghouls.

Mini haunted house

STEP 1
Stick together a variety of cardboard boxes using PVA glue.

STEP 2
Paint the whole thing with grey acrylic paint.

STEP 3
Using semi-circles of coloured paper make cones and stick them to the tops of the boxes.

STEP 4
Add paper windows and doors to decorate. Make some white card ghosts and stick them to the walls.

 **TOP TIP!**

Go large! Make a big scale version of this haunted house out of larger boxes.

HALLOWEEN BUNTING

YOU WILL NEED:

- construction paper (orange and black for pumpkins, white and black for ghosts)
- crayons or marker pens
- scissors
- a long piece of green or black yarn or string
- sticky tape / stapler

STEP 1

Draw a jack-o'-lantern's face on a piece of orange paper, and a ghost on white paper. Draw a long stem on the top of each one (your pumpkin or ghost will hang from this stem, which will be folded over).

stem

stem

STEP 2

Cut out the pumpkin or ghost. Draw eyes and a mouth. Fold the pumpkin's stem in half. Fold the ghost's stem completely behind the ghost.

fold here

fold here

STEP 3

Attach the pumpkin or ghost to a long piece of coloured string using tape or staples.

staple or tape here

staple or tape here

Did you KNOW?

In China they celebrate the Hungry Ghost Festival which happens on the 15th night of the 7th month. This month of the Chinese calendar is thought to be the spookiest time where the ghosts are let out of hell to roam the country, trying to cause trouble.

ZOMBIE GRAVEYARD

People will be dying to join you at your zombie-themed party! Create a spooky atmosphere by making these jam jar lanterns to light up your gruesome gravestones.

Graveyard lanterns

YOU WILL NEED:

- scrap card
- pencil
- empty, clean jam jar
- glass paints
- pain brush
- 60 cm of garden wire
- LED light

STEP 1

Draw a graveyard scene on a scrap of card with lots of graves, and hanging trees.

STEP 2

Roll the scene up and put it inside the jar.

put card in jar

STEP 3

Use the paper scene as a template for you to trace. Use glass paints to colour in the design directly onto the glass. Then remove the card and leave to dry.

STEP 4

Bend the wire around the neck of the jar and twist to join it together. Bend the long end over the top to form the handle and feed under the wire, bending upwards to fix.

STEP 5

Put in the LED light.

What did one zombie say to the other zombie when they were eating a comedian?
This tastes funny!

Salt dough tombstones

YOU WILL NEED:
- 1 cup of salt
- 2 cups of flour
- water
- black food colouring
- margarine lid
- craft glue
- soil
- black marker pen

FLOUR

SALT

1. Mix one cup of salt with two cups of flour.

2. Add one cup of water and mix to make a dough. Add a few drops of black food colouring to dye it grey.

3. Mould your dough into a tombstone shape and a hand. Ask an adult to bake them in an oven at 60°C until the dough is dry. This will take about three hours.

4. Use the black marker pen to decorate the tombstone with a cross.

5. Glue the tombstone and hand onto the margarine lid and sprinkle soil to cover the rest of the lid.

DRACULA'S CASTLE

Do you know the story of Count Dracula? He lived in a castle in Transylvania where he slept all day in a coffin to avoid the sunlight. He could instantly turn into a bat and fly around to find his next victim.

Pom-pom bats

YOU WILL NEED:
- black tissue paper
- pencil
- scissors
- needle and thread
- large bead
- scrap paper
- googly eyes
- craft glue

STEP 1
Fold the tissue paper in half many times until you have several layers of folded paper.

STEP 2
Draw a flower shape onto the top with a pencil. Cut this shape out so you have lots of the same shape. Make 15 shapes in total.

STEP 3
Use a needle to thread a large round bead onto some thread and then add the paper flowers by pushing the needle through the centre of each.

needle →

STEP 4
Tie a knot above the paper flowers and then tie a loop with the leftover thread.

STEP 5
Fluff out the shapes to make the pom-pom shape and decorate with paper wings and fangs, and a pair of googly eyes.

Coffin candy tray

YOU WILL NEED:
- brown card
- scissors
- ruler
- sticky tape
- gold pen
- red fabric
- craft glue
- sweets

STEP 1
Cut two coffin shapes and two 5-cm-wide strips from brown card. Stick the strip around the edge of one coffin shape with tape.

tape here

tape here

STEP 2
Attach on the lid to one side of the coffin box with tape.

tape here

tape here

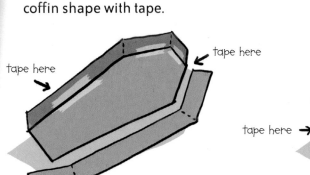

STEP 3
Use the gold pen to decorate the outside of the coffin, including a cross and fancy hinges.

Why did Dracula take cold medicine?
To stop his coffin!

Did you KNOW?

The tales of Dracula are based on a real man, Vlad the Impaler who ruled Wallachia, now Romania, in the 15th century. He changed his name to Dracula, after his father Dracul, which means 'Son of the Dragon'.

STEP 4
Glue the red fabric inside the box to decorate it, then fill with sweets.

MONSTER MASH BALL

Inspired by the tales of Frankenstein and his monster, invite other monsters to your ball, which you can hold in your dark and dusty basement laboratory.

Felt monsters

YOU WILL NEED:
- pencil
- thin card
- scissors
- coloured felt
- needle and thread
- toy stuffing
- fabric glue

STEP 1
Draw a monster silhouette onto a piece of thin card. Cut out to make a template.

STEP 2
Use the template to cut out two identical shapes from the piece of coloured felt.

STEP 3
Sew the two shapes together, making sure you leave a small gap on the side.

leave gap

STEP 4
Stuff the shape with the toy stuffing and sew up the gap.

fill with stuffing

STEP 5
Cut out shapes from the other pieces of coloured felt to make eyes, teeth and horns. Stick them onto the monster's body using the fabric glue.

☞ TOP TIP!

You can decorate any surface with these cute monsters. Pin names onto them to turn them into name place settings or sew on some ribbon so they can hang from the ceiling.

 **TOP TIP!**

Make your basement look extra spooky by making lots of these spider webs and sticking them on the walls. You can scrunch up balls of coloured tissue paper with pipe cleaner legs to make spiders to hang from the webs too!

GLITTERY SPIDER'S WEB

YOU WILL NEED:
- old newspaper
- black paper
- glue
- glitter

STEP 1
Working on old newspaper, draw a spider web with glue on the black construction paper. Start by drawing a series of intersecting lines.

STEP 2
After drawing the intersecting lines, draw the curved lines between them. Work quickly before the glue dries.

STEP 3
Sprinkle glitter on the glue web. Gently shake the picture and let the excess glitter slide off the spider web (onto the newspaper).

Did you KNOW?

Many people think that the green creature you see about at Halloween is called Frankenstein, but it's actually the name of its creator, Victor Frankenstein. The famous book by Mary Shelley tells the story of a young scientist who makes a monster which he never names.

POEMS

Trick or treat! Trick or treat!
Give us something good to eat
Fill our bellies with things
that are yummy
'Til we moan that we have
a sore tummy.

Trick or treat! Trick or treat!
Give us something good to eat.
Chocolates and sweets in all
shapes and sizes,
So many treats I can't believe
my eyes.

Trick or treat! Trick or treat!
Give us something good to eat.
What about the tricks that are
in store
From the people who live just
behind this door?

What is a vampire's
favourite fruit?

A nectarine!

Ghost and ghouls and witches galore
So many spooks you've not seen before
Around every corner are things that will scare
So enter this haunted house if you dare.
It's only for those who can last the night
and cope with the monsters that like to fright
But all this must be made up for one scary day
Ghosts, ghouls and witches don't exist ...
do they?

There once was a zombie called Vince
and people around him would wince.
His breath was so bad
from all the brains that he'd had
That he switched to eating packets
of mints.

On Halloween all the
ghosts to come out to play
It's their favourite
festival or so they say
To spook and scare the
passers-by
When it gets dark and stars
fill the sky
But we all know...

QUIZ

How much do you really know about Halloween? Test your knowledge and see if you can answer all ten questions correctly. Don't be scared: all the answers can be found in this book!

1. The first jack-o'-lanterns were originally made from which vegetable?

2. Which Celtic festival is Halloween thought to have come from?

3. What was the night before All Hallows' Day called?

4. In which American state can you find the Bell Witch Cave?

5. What is the name of the cake that is given out during souling?

6. Who wrote the book about Victor Frankenstein?

7. What two colours, popular at Halloween, came from the pagan festival for autumn and the harvest?

8. What Mexican holiday is celebrated around Halloween?

9. Which popular Halloween character came from the Samhain celebration that honoured a pagan goddess called the Crone?

10. Which Scottish tradition is thought to have inspired trick-or-treating, where children go from house to house in disguise?

GLOSSARY

Christian Someone who follows the teachings of Jesus Christ.

commemorate To remember and show respect for someone.

devil The most powerful evil spirit in some religions.

disguise Using a costume to change your appearance and hide your identity.

fondant icing A thick icing paste made from sugar and water.

ghoul An evil spirit that is said to like to enjoy eating dead bodies.

harvest The time of the year where crops are collected from fields.

immigrant A person who has come to live permanently in a country that is not their own.

jagged Something with sharp pointed edges.

laboratory A room used for scientific research and experiments.

legend A very old and popular story that may or may not be true.

medieval The period of European history between 476 and about 1500.

pagan A word that describes a range of ancient groups who usually worship many gods, nature and the sun.

soul The part of a person that consists of your mind, thoughts, and feelings; believed to exist after death.

spirit A ghost or the part of a person that is believed to remain alive after their death.

stalactites These are icicle-like structures that can often be found hanging in caves.

sugar skull An edible skull made from sugar and decorated with colourful patterns like flowers and hearts.

translucent Material that light can pass through, but you can't see through.

QUIZ ANSWERS

1. Turnips
2. Samhain
3. All Hallows' Eve
4. Tennessee
5. Soul Cake
6. Mary Shelley
7. Orange and black
8. Day of the Dead
9. A witch
10. Guising

31

INDEX